Beauty in
DISREPAIR

NORMA *and* CELIA FORTE

ARCHWAY PUBLISHING

Copyright © 2020 Norma and Celia Forte.

All rights reserved. No part of this book may be used or reproduced by any means, graphic, electronic, or mechanical, including photocopying, recording, taping or by any information storage retrieval system without the written permission of the author except in the case of brief quotations embodied in critical articles and reviews.

This book is a work of non-fiction. Unless otherwise noted, the author and the publisher make no explicit guarantees as to the accuracy of the information contained in this book and in some cases, names of people and places have been altered to protect their privacy.

Archway Publishing books may be ordered through booksellers or by contacting:

Archway Publishing
1663 Liberty Drive
Bloomington, IN 47403
www.archwaypublishing.com
844-669-3957

Because of the dynamic nature of the Internet, any web addresses or links contained in this book may have changed since publication and may no longer be valid. The views expressed in this work are solely those of the author and do not necessarily reflect the views of the publisher, and the publisher hereby disclaims any responsibility for them.

Any people depicted in stock imagery provided by Getty Images are models, and such images are being used for illustrative purposes only. Certain stock imagery © Getty Images.

Scripture quotations are taken from the King James Version.

ISBN: 978-1-4808-9713-7 (sc)
ISBN: 978-1-4808-9714-4 (e)

Library of Congress Control Number: 2020919086

Print information available on the last page.

Archway Publishing rev. date: 10/15/2020

CONTENTS

Dedication vii

Preface: A Note to Readers ix

Introduction xiii
   At Grandma's Home xiii
   The Youngest xiv
   The Oldest xvi

Chapter 1: Home and Health in Disrepair 1
   The Cold Room 1
   Mother 2
   Breakfast 4
   Jelly, Mayo, and Bread 6
   Food Desert 9
   Lemonade Stand 10
   Mom's Men 12
   Lonely 14
   Shit-Kickers 16
   Triggers 18
   Boot Camp 19
   Happy Birthday 20
   Order is Safe 23
   Playtime 25
   Uncertainty 26
   Cleanliness 28
   Hypochondria 30
   Sick 31
   Oxygen Supply 34
   Alters at Odds 35

Chapter 2: Religion and Faith in Disrepair 37
   Hallelujah 37
   I Believe 38
   Sacred Space 39

 Speaking in Tongues 40
 A Witch 42
 The Zealot 43
 Possessed 50

Chapter 3: Sexuality in Disrepair 53
 I Keep the Light On 53
 His Power 54
 Come to Me 55
 Dirty Girl 57
 What Do You Tell Your Friends? 59
 Thunder and Enlightening 61

Our Final Thoughts 63
 Mom 63
 The Youngest 66
 The Oldest 68

A Poem by Our Mom 71
 He Asked Me to Say My Prayer 71

DEDICATION

We dedicate this book in the memory of our mother, who suffered with Dissociative Identity Disorder and did the best that she could to raise us through mental illness, poverty, and chaos. To the best of our recollection, this poetry and prose reflects our childhood as survivors of direct abuse and the residual effects of DID. It is hard to imagine what it must have felt like for her when she shifted between personalities—how strange she must have felt peering in the mirror at someone she did not always recognize or choose to see. We take comfort that in her death, we made peace and her remains were set to rest in gentle streams and winding trails where finally, she was made whole.

-Sisters

PREFACE: A NOTE TO READERS

This collection of poetry and prose is a joint memoir. Over the years we have poured over legal and medical records, as well as collected some reference materials from family and friends who knew our mother. As confusing as Dissociative Identity Disorder was for us as children, it must have been even more so for her. In the spirit of understanding how disjointed it felt growing up in a home with someone who had DID (multiple personality disorder), we have adopted a stylistic approach of a collage; we have mixed poetry and prose with two very different voices throughout. Life was a kaleidoscope, but the images weren't always beautiful. Her mind was intelligent and insightful, but as the alter personalities surfaced, all were in a state of disrepair. We lived it in some form every day growing up in the ever-changing face of our mother. By the time we were contacted by her psychiatrist, she had been diagnosed with twenty-two alters.

Those alters ranged in age, gender, race, and temperament. A person with the diagnosis of Dissociative Identity Disorder uses these personalities as coping skills to deal with certain feelings and situations in which s/he may feel cornered, threatened, or shy. There are many theories as to why this happens, but the most widely accepted is that trauma, usually physical or sexual, initially separates the original alter one is born with and the fractures continue to grow as time progresses. She had a variety of alters: children, teenagers, men, protectors, instigators, addicts, abusers, as well as her birth alter.

For those who have heard of Dissociative Identity Disorder, the misconception is that it is much like the films, television programs, or documentaries and books depict. That is rarely the case. In fact, children who survive experiences with violent personalities associated with the disorder endure far worse and the effects are residual throughout adulthood. We chose to construct this book with readers in mind, and to try to relay memories that for so long, have devoured our sense of our dignity, self-worth, and success. We decided that to get through our past and what happened to us, that we do not remain victims, but rather, survivors who see a future that allows for forgiveness, even though we will never forget what happened to us.

Our mother unfortunately was abused as a toddler, although the identity of the individual is still unknown. In those days, children played outside together with little fear of harm. Times were simpler and safer. At least that was true for others, but not for Mom. Her psychiatrists gathered that she was raped at the age of three-years-old. This makes sense because some of her personalities were small children; I recount visiting her years later to find dolls and other toys hidden around her apartment for when those alters were present. When she could "come out" as her birth alter, she was kind, generous, artistic, intelligent, funny, and beautiful. But when her eyes darkened, or her facial expression or voice changed, we knew that *she* had left and someone else, often someone angry, took her place.

She showed signs of mental illness in childhood, but in high school she became more erratic. By nature, she was a bit shyer and more reserved, but there was another side of her that was very outgoing. High school years were good for her; she enjoyed her studies, flourished socially, and had a plethora of activities to engage her. But with each trial or trigger, the personalities gathered momentum and became apparent more often. Once she had children, she already had at least one or two very angry, abusive personalities. One alter, was the most pronounced and active abuser. She was mom's protector and our abuser. The personalities grew to be so developed, that one of them, an older man, caused her to shave her head completely. When a younger alter presented itself, the clothing she purchased was trendy and stylish and her attitude was upbeat and full of happiness. These are only several of the twenty-two alters she held in her mind. How exhausting. How she suffered.

It has taken most of our adulthood, but we have come to terms with forgiveness. Nevertheless, to forget is altogether a different thing. It requires attempting to uproot and to rid ourselves of the past—erasure of it all. Unless we cope and forgive, we cannot move forward. But to forget, well, there is far too much that we have learned from these experiences to discount them completely. There will always be flashbacks and nightmares, distrust, and anger, but at least we understand why she did these things to us. She was ill. She tried to make herself well with education, religion, sex, shopping, eating disorders, relationships, work—but she could not cure herself. Her counsellors did their best to integrate the alters, but in the end when she died, we believe the alters united or merged. The pain of these memories will get better, but not before it hurts, a lot. A cut heals because it goes through the painful process of fighting infection and regenerating skin. If our bodies heal this way, then maybe our minds can, too.

~Sisters

INTRODUCTION

AT GRANDMA'S HOME
CELIA

Remember sneaking into her room
on tiptoes? Wondering if it was
safe—if we'd get caught
this time?

How good it felt to each
pull an end of the
enormous drawer until it
creaked open.

Crinkle of yellowing paper,
Grandpa's letters …
love. Empty perfume bottles—still
scented. Strings of costume jewelry—
faux, but beautiful because hers.
How smooth the pearls felt?
How musty the box was! Pictures of them
smiling shyly, her hand in his.

Each of us promised sweet-sixteen treasures—
we couldn't wait. We loved stealing into her room,
she in the garden, you tugging my shirt to get a peek.
We touched the jewels, papers, bottles until

the screen door squeaked open and slammed
shut as we clumsily pushed the drawer halfway.
Remember how we laughed to hear her say,
Who's been poking through my drawer?

THE YOUNGEST
NORMA

My life comes to me as a jumble of pictures and words. Sometimes the pictures are whole, sometimes the pictures are in pieces. Sometimes it's like putting together a puzzle, but it's not a fun puzzle or a puzzle in the Sunday paper; it's a puzzle that I don't want the answer to. I look at it like a broken mirror, a mirror in which somebody took a hammer. The bigger pieces remained on the outside holding the smaller ones in. As I move closer to the center, the mirror is in fragments. Some of those pieces lay outside of the mirror below it. I try to put the pieces back in, but I'm afraid of getting cut. So far, this is what I've been able to reframe.

My mother was in her early twenties when she had me. At that time, she was already the mother of a six-year-old girl. My father was her second husband. Her first marriage had ended badly. If that marriage had ended badly then her second marriage to my biological father would have been beyond words. Everything that my mother said to me had to be taken with a grain of salt. I couldn't always trust the things that came out of her mouth; some were lies some were half-truths; some were blatant misconfigurations of the world around her. Sometimes she saw the world as an enemy when it was trying to hold her hand. Sometimes who she saw as friends were only there to take advantage of her. But one thing I did know after reading many police reports and documents from doctors, teachers and lawyers was that my father was a monster. There are many instances of abuse that he put our family through: beatings, stabbings, and instances of sexual trauma and verbal assaults. These things he did not only to my sister and I, but mostly to my mother. After an especially brutal assault in which my father took a baseball bat to my mother and broke many bones in her body, disfigured her face and left her for dead, my mother gathered enough courage to take us two children and run. She never went back, although the damage that my father did to our family could never be undone.

I was too young to remember that day. I had been told the story many times by my mother and sister. Sometimes I was glad that I could not remember, sometimes I wish that I could, but I always felt guilty. I was a toddler when my mother left my father and there is no way that I could have helped the situation at that age, but I always took it on as "my father, my fault." That is a stigma that I carry with me to this day. Although I don't remember my earliest years, most recollections come to me by way of a smell or a song. Small flashes and glimpses which come and go. The pieces, they grow bigger and bigger as I get older and I am better able to put them together.

THE OLDEST
CELIA

When I discuss some of the things that happened in my childhood, I am usually met with disbelief. People seem to think I have it all figured out and that I am a person who has it "together." I have a good career and a husband who is loyal and supportive. But what people cannot see is the constant racing of my mind, the constant firing of neurotransmitters that never seem to settle—not even in slumber. As an insomniac, I have tried everything to fall asleep. I have wandered local roads late at night, trying to fatigue my body ... but the mind never relents. Because of the chaos in my head, my environment must be ordered. Those who visit my office will immediately notice my obsessive-compulsive tendencies: clean desk, books in order of genre, symmetry of artwork, and not a pen out of place. The same is true of my home. Perhaps this is due to constant relocations in childhood; we moved a lot, along with Mom's personalities/alters or my stepfather's military service, and often changed schools and sold all our belongings to start over each time. Order is essential for me now and I have learned to avoid attachments to material belongings; I also tread carefully in personal relationships because we never knew when or where we would relocate, and it was better to guard my heart. The only place that gave me any sense of comfort was our maternal grandmother's home—as I discussed in the poem above—although there were times when Mom kept us from family for months or even years. We knew when we were at our grandmother's house, we would be fed well, could wash our clothes in a washing machine instead of the bathtub, and we were protected from Mom's personality shifts.

In addition to feeling unsettled as a child and adolescent, there was abuse in all forms inflicted on my sister and me. For readers who had stable family lives, ours will seem like a nightmare. After all, how did we survive all these instances relayed in this book? Not only was Mom suffering from mental illness, but our biological fathers were not part of our upbringing in the formative years—not really. Both served in the military, one was diagnosed with Schizophrenia, the other clearly struggled with PTSD (Post Traumatic Stress Disorder). It will be difficult to imagine a childhood as confusing and unstable as ours as one reads this book. There have been many books and films written about all these disorders that our parents have suffered through, but none have captured how we felt as children living through it. And so, we hope that this book does reach the children who have survived as we have, and that in some small way, others will step out of the darkness and hopelessness that survivors experience.

We now know that DID is caused by traumatic events, which differ in degree and may or may not be the result of parental abuse. I often wonder how we even survived our childhood, but then I think back on the many people who stepped in when they could to help or comfort us. As children, there was little known about these disorders then, and school nurses had limited resources for reporting (and we were threatened that if we ever told anyone about what went on at home, that we would "get it" much worse when we returned from school or other activities). The cycle of abuse continued beyond our adolescence; as such, my sister and I both have endured abusive and/or unhealthy relationships in our adolescent and adult lives. Finally, we are both happily married, but our insecurities often rear their ugliness and we are both fortunate to have people in our lives that can tolerate and calm our own disorders.

Still, the repercussions of living with such turmoil for most of our lives has left us often emotionally depleted, sexually, and physically challenged, and socially and spiritually scarred. It is a constant fight for both of us to tread water in a pool of depression and anxiety, which are a deadly mixture when combined with memories of our childhood. We have both been to the dark place, the place where we feel the best thing for everyone would be for us to just disappear. For me, there is residual guilt for having left my sister with Mom when I moved in with my father. My rational mind knows that it was critical for me to get away from Mom, but as a teenager, I could not provide for my sister. Later, my sister earned an early high school diploma and an early admission to college. Somehow, over time, through counselling and with others' help, we are healthier now and functioning as "productively" as possible. We hope others that lived through similar experiences can see how we endured and found acceptance, love, and hope.

Chapter 1
HOME AND HEALTH IN DISREPAIR

THE COLD ROOM
CELIA

Secrets in the closet in the cold room,
their bedroom, dark and damp, full gloom—

had been the one forbidden as a child,
which led my imagination into wild

fantasies of corpses, treasures—secrets.
I'd sneak in while they played croquet

with the neighbors, who probably knew
what lay in the darkness, breeding mildew.

The contents of boxes I'd never see, since
someone caught me turning the knob—

it was never locked. Did they want me to uncover
the years of shame, memories that hovered

over and kept them in whispers long into night?
After they'd tuck me in, I'd crawl to see the light
under the door. My ear pressed hard on wood,
I'd listen, though I could never hear what I should.

I should have heard what was in those
boxes. The ghosts needed to be loosed.

I never found what was in that closet, the room so cold.
The house, now empty—dark and damp—has since been sold.

Beauty in Disrepair

MOTHER

NORMA

After finishing high school a year early, I was accepted into a local state university. Although just across town, I chose to leave home and stay in the dormitories on campus. During this time, another shift in my mother occurred.

Her clothing became more stylish, her hair, a shorter, brighter color, and her voice, a higher pitch. She started dating one of my acquaintances, not much older than me. She got her first tattoo. I thought at first that she was trying to be like me so that she wouldn't be left behind. I didn't know if this was a new personality that was filling in the void of me leaving and grieving her empty nest or if this was an old personality that was happy its freedom had finally returned. Either way, I was now the new keeper of a teenage mother.

When I look back now, I remember other times that this younger person seemed to be in control. Obsessive shopping sprees that left us without grocery money. Random men, there for a night and then gone forever. Messy closets and clothes that were too tight. An abundance of shoes and purses, but never enough in the cupboard for both of us to eat.

I learned to make something from nothing for dinner a lot of the times. Using blends of years-old spices that sat on the shelf to come up with broths that were halfway decent. I drank water like it was going out of style. I walked down to the bakery outlet that was a couple of blocks away and bought the animal feed they had; items that were a week or more past date. I could empty these boxes of doughnuts, cakes, and pies into a huge plastic bag for nineteen cents a pound. I hauled this plastic sack of food back home like a dejected and hungry Santa Claus. There I spent time cutting off the crusty and moldy parts of the food and put it in the freezer to make it last.

My mother's teenage personalities spent a lot of money on makeup, clothing, and things of little importance. She was constantly bringing home things for "me," yet they were always in her size. New shoes and pizza meant we wouldn't eat for the rest of the week. It seemed we were always behind the game. I didn't realize how far behind until I left home and discovered my credit score had been demolished because of all the accounts posted in my name.

Other changes were more than subtle. Halfway through my first year at college, my grandmother died. I was notified of this by two police officers showing up at my dorm room. While the other hall residents looked on, they told me that my grandmother had just died. I hadn't time to grieve. I fell against the door and the officer grabbed my hand to hold it and he said, "Honey, we need to take you to your mom. She's losing it."

I rode back to our apartment in the back of a police cruiser preparing for what I would find when I got back home. Two more officers were at her apartment trying to keep her calm. When they were sure I would be okay, they left. Through the tears, my mother looked at me and said in a soft, sweet voice, "My mommy died."

"I know," I said, and I held her tight.

I spent a couple of days with her, helping her pack a couple of bags to take on the trip home after the funeral. While she was gone, I stayed at her apartment to watch it. I decided to snoop, and I'm glad I did. I was able to find the police reports against my father, hospital reports about my mother, and court and church records that substantiated quite a few of my mother's recollections.

BREAKFAST

NORMA

I could hear the sounds of the other kids playing outside. I just didn't want to be left out. The uncontrollable laughter, the sounds of bicycle chains and water hoses. I was already in my swimsuit; I had put it on as soon as I had gotten up in the morning because I knew today was going to be a day of playing outside. We lived on a block where all the children played together when playing outside from sunup to sundown was the normal thing to do. My sister and I found freedom in playing outside with the other kids; it meant we were not inside the house all day with my mother. There were children my sister's age and there were children my age, although there are six years that separate the two of us. I sat at the table listening to the other kids play outside.

My sister and I were eating our breakfasts. Eggs, toast, and orange juice. The eggs were over easy and slightly runny around the yolk. I ate my egg and I dipped my toast into the yolk, but I couldn't bring myself to eat the runny white part. My mother repeatedly told me if I didn't eat what was on my plate I couldn't go out and play. So, I kept eating right around the egg until the runny white was all that was left, but that still wasn't good enough for her. I gathered up a piece of slime on my fork and put it in my mouth. I couldn't get myself to chew or swallow it. I just remember the feeling of the cold, wet slime up against the roof of my mouth. That funny feeling that one gets when holding back tears that sends water running through the jaws and tingling up the sides of the face was taking over. I was trying to hang on but couldn't hold back the tears for too long.

My sister sat across the table from me, and I remember her looking at me like she wanted to be able to do something but knew that she could not. My mother came back into the room to find me still holding the slime in my mouth and said, "Eat your goddamn food." I was crying and I told her that I couldn't. She smacked me hard across the face.

"Eat your fucking food or you're not going outside!" she yelled at me. The smack made me choke on the piece that was in my mouth and it slid down the back of my throat, leaving me retching. At that moment I knew this was it, and every bite that I had managed to get in my stomach came back up as I vomited all over my plate. My mother walked behind me and hit me hard in the back of the head.

"Do you think you're going to get out of it now?" she yelled. "I said you have to eat everything on your plate or you're not going outside to play."

I looked at my plate and I looked back at her. Even at seven I knew exactly what this meant. My mother yelled at my sister and told her to go on and play. My heart sank; she was going to be outside. It took me hours, but I ate everything on my plate.

JELLY, MAYO, AND BREAD

CELIA

For as long as I can remember, food was always scarce in my mother's house. Somehow, we always had enough condiments, but almost never any proteins to accompany them. What she always had in stock were crackers that scratched the roof of my mouth and diet chewy candies, which I thought were actual chocolate. I hated those crackers, and to this day I never buy them, as they had no flavor and broke into tiny pieces everywhere. I still hate grape jelly. We always had a huge jar of it. I do not even think that Mom liked the stuff, but we always had plenty. Luckily, the nice young neighbor downstairs was a hippie with a gentle spirit. She baked her own bread, lived a quiet, nature-loving life, and always welcomed my visits for fresh bread and butter. I loved those afternoons. Sometimes the neighbor upstairs, a middle-aged woman who knew our grandmother, practiced her religious faith by giving us food when we needed it. Our grandpa walked across town to our apartment (he never drove) to bring us groceries too. Those moments of charity were short-lived, as Mom ultimately cut off friends and family by causing drama in some way. Back then, I did not understand why we could not see my grandparents, why I could not visit the neighbors anymore, or why Mom was so unpredictable.

I am sure that if we had been tested for malnutrition, my sister and I would have been iron deficient (Mom often vacillated between being a vegetarian and a carnivore). Perhaps our calcium intake was too low, and very often, we didn't have enough fresh produce or healthy grains. I recall countless boxes of dried milk, huge logs of clay-like government cheese, and big tins of oily peanut butter. None of those items tasted like what we ate from the store or Gram's kitchen—in fact, there was little distinction in flavor between those items. As I grew into my pre-teen years, I noticed that when Mom came into any money at all, she bought an extravagant meal for the three of us, and of course purchased a few "cute" purses, scarves, or other accessory items for herself. I now know that it was probably one of her alters that behaved so irresponsibly with the little money we had at any given time in our youth, because our Mom, the birth alter, would never choose something for herself over others.

But that is the complexity of this disorder—that the alters behave much differently than the original birth personality. Mom clearly suffered from body dysmorphic disorder, too, always obsessed with her weight and ours, often skipping meals (which I still do) and immediately retreating to the bathroom right after eating something heavy (which I have done). I recall standing in the hallway hearing her wretch repeatedly, then the swish of the toilet, then the cold water splashing over her face. She emerged with eyes red-rimmed and dabbing the sides of her mouth. I learned in later years that I could either live on chocolate milk on lunch breaks at school, not eat at all, or binge and get rid of it all to stay slim.

As I grew older, I began to focus on exercise—vehemently. I did countless reps of sit-ups, calisthenics, and stretches in my room. Then I began working out religiously in various gyms. I became a woman obsessed, who tabulated everything I ate as I lay in bed at night—a visual image like counting sheep only to fall into restless dreams that ignited my nightmares. As a result of these patterned behaviors, I later became obsessed with food in another way. I began to research and to eat voraciously, trying anything new that I could stomach by creating my own recipes, and I found that food had become a joyful passion. But that enjoyment has always come with a price. The guilt I feel after eating is ever present. Even now, I still struggle with food consumption, preparation, and calculation, but at least I am not as obsessed with immediately exercising to rid myself of the excesses of that passion.

Now, I simply hoard food. I grow very nervous when my freezer isn't stocked to full capacity, or when my fridge shelves hold few items. My cupboards—the same. I am happiest when I am fully stocked at home and grow uneasy when our supply is low. My sister struggles with this, too, and she and I believe that if there are onions and maybe a bag of rice, one can do wonders. We have learned to make good food out of few resources, and both ended up spending much of our twenties in the restaurant industry. We have, possibly without realizing it all those years, surrounded ourselves with food sources: food pantries when we were young were frequently visited;

buffets at restaurants were our favorite—felt like what an opiate addict must feel in a pharmacy; and we worked in the food industry. One positive outcome of this love/hate relationship with food is that we are both generous with sharing it. I am not sure that had we not gone without for so long, that we would be as cognizant as we are of how others may need necessities like food. It always amazes me how fragile we are as human beings, but how strong the collective human spirit can be if we only learn from the past, embrace the future, and by all means, share a lot of meals together—as long as it isn't government issued food or crackers with grape jelly, or as we sometimes ate, mayonnaise on bread.

FOOD DESERT
NORMA

As my group of friends started to include me in things outside of school, I started to see how most families interacted. What I perceived to be normal was in fact nowhere near what other kids my age were going through. Teenagers had boyfriends. School dances weren't orgies. Running down the street and doing summersaults was completely normal.

One thing that completely shocked me was the availability of food in other households. I had one friend who I would walk to school and home with many days of the week. We had stopped at her home after school and she went to her freezer, pulled out a bag of French fries and started prepping them for the oven. I was shocked.

How was she able to eat without asking for permission? Especially since the preparation included using the oven. Using the oven took electricity and electricity cost money. I was dumbfounded. She had emptied half the bag of French fries onto the baking sheet. That wasn't a snack, that was a meal! I was hoping for her sake that her parents weren't home. I didn't want her to get in trouble. What I thought was normal was nowhere near it.

When the fries came out of the oven, she asked if I wanted any. I had to weigh this very carefully, I was hungry, but that would mean I ate when Mom didn't and that wasn't fair. I could have just a couple, but would that make me smell like fries? I didn't care. I was going for it. I took a handful of fries and ate. They were delicious.

As things like this began to happen, I started to engage with the outside world more and more. I opened little by little and started to learn my worth. In other homes I saw that friends were allowed to come and go. No one was trying to hide anything. Friends could even talk about whatever they wanted to, and the parents would talk to them without fluctuation, exasperation, or exaggeration. I noticed the lack of tension and drama. When I saw parents fight, there wouldn't be screaming and when I saw parents fight with children there wouldn't be any harm. I wonder if my ignorance at these situations was obvious on my face. Could people tell how lost I was?

LEMONADE STAND
CELIA

I recall one instance in which we lived in a second-floor apartment while Mom worked on her college degree. The children in the building often played, running up and down stairs, creating our own little worlds, making our own dollhouses, and selling lemonade out of the basement playroom. There was a little sliding window that we could "do drive-thru" out of and we really enjoyed the prospect of making some cash to buy the newest shoes, toys, or books that were popular at the time. But every neighborhood has bullies, and I was the lucky recipient of their attention. I was mocked on the school bus, and sometimes chased through the snow as I tried to get to the safety of our babysitter's house. I remember being tripped, whitewashed (for those who do not know the term, it is a pile of snow and ice smashed into one's face), and chased every day I jumped off the bus steps—a dead run almost immediately upon hitting the ground.

These bullies lived right across the street and when they came to our lemonade stand, we begrudgingly sold them some. Instead of drinking it down, they splashed the acidic drink into my friend's eyes. As she screamed and ran to her apartment to splash her face, I told Mom. Since there was no father in the picture at this time, we had to rely on only Mom. While she calmed us down (she was her birth alter on this day—no personality shifts) and we played a new game, shutting down our little business for good. Days later the boys still taunted us, throwing tiny rocks at our bedroom window, yelling at us. This triggered something in our mother as she stood erect, pursed her lips into a tight bow, and then punched her fist through the window.

I do not recall the blood, nor do I recall the shattered glass along the floorboards. What I do recall is the confusion on my sister's face, the panic in my bones, and the resolve of my mother's threat. She hollered out the window such obscenities that even the boys below (who surely knew a few of their own) scattered. They ran to their home even as Mom continued to degrade them. This was one of the instances by which her force was not doled out to either my sister or I; instead, she attempted to scare off and protect us from bullies. The irony is not lost here, because Mom was usually the biggest bully of all.

MOM'S MEN
CELIA

Our fathers were absent even when present, not there to protect and in some cases, one was the abuser of both of us. These men had issues of their own and this book is less about them and really about our experiences with our mother, our primary caregiver. It is important to note, though, that neither father was able to parent due to their own issues and the first memory of my biological father is the day my parents separated. I recall Mom and I curled up on the couch together under a blanket, and I remember he said he loved me as he shut the apartment door. That is a child's memory with an adult's acceptance and forgiveness.

Absent, present—either way, we had no fathers in childhood. When Mom was married to her second husband, my biological father had long since been out of the picture. My stepfather was violent and degrading. I often wanted to escape their fighting and feared that I would be caught in the middle. I had begged to play outside that day, as there was a group of kids in the apartment complex that were shrieking and laughing with excitement as they played tag, hung upside down on the monkey bars, and sang childhood ditties: "Ring around the Rosy," "Nanny, Nanny Boo-Boo," mostly taunting tunes. I recall paisley curtains playing peekaboo as parents checked on their shrieking kids occasionally from the comfort of their polyester world. As I begged to go outside, Mom begged me to stay inside. She knew that the chances of her receiving a solid beating were slimmer if I was around. But I was a selfish child and wanted to play with the other children. She finally relented, and her fears were confirmed.

As I climbed the monkey bars and swung my legs up, I hooked my ankles under the next bar and let my body hang upside down. I enjoyed the feeling of the blood rushing to my head. I could smell the sweetness of freshly mowed lawns and the children around me were as drunk on the summer freedom as I. No school. Just play. As I swung my body upwards again, I decided to hop on a vacant swing next. I made my way, began pumping my legs, and as I rose higher and higher someone yelled, "Pump your legs more!" I felt elated. Nothing could touch me when I was that high in the air. Not even my stepfather could reach me there. I was flying. Nevertheless, that moment was short-lived, as the unmistakable screams of my mother carried out the window, echoed over the balcony, and hung over the playground. The children around me began to look toward the sound, which was now accompanied by breaking furniture and smashing glass. But I was a child and instead of being concerned for my mother's safety, I was angry. *How dare they embarrass me like this!* All the children began to whip their necks back and forth as if watching a perverse tennis match—they just kept swinging their eyes between our balcony and me, still flying so high no one could catch me. As the sounds increased, the children began to disperse. The abuse was so unbridled—so physically charged, that the neighbors began to come out of their homes to collect their children. Those too afraid continued to play peekaboo behind the paisley. Eventually, I was alone on the playground. I was embarrassed that everyone knew the family secret. I was ashamed that people knew my stepfather beat my mother. More than that, I was ashamed that I was so selfish for wanting to avoid that shit storm called home.

LONELY
CELIA

I often made up sign language hand motions and pretended that I was communicating with a schoolmate, who was hearing impaired. I wasn't making fun of her but felt comfortable around her; I felt safe and different like her, because I knew my home was not like other children's homes. I was so very shy, and she welcomed me into her little circle of friends during recess. I recall when the bell rang to go back inside, that I motioned to her and she corralled her friends to go as I walked after them. I felt a part of something. I felt less alone at school.

When at home, I had imaginary friends until one day I met a girl on the playground, and we became playmates. She looked a lot like a doll I owned and loved, and I suppose that is what drew me to her initially. We were stationed in a complex for military families. My only friend seemed as lost as I was—constantly moving and starting over in new schools. My friend had so many freckles and was shy like me. She came to our apartment to play dolls one day, but she did not stay long. My stepfather came home and almost immediately, he and Mom entered a verbal sparring match, which was soon to become physical. It always did.

My little friend stood up, wide-eyed, and said, "I have to go now."

I begged her to stay, but I would have gone with her if I could have; I did not want to go through this again by myself. My sister was just a toddler and I felt so lonely with no one my age to talk to or to play with and I knew what was coming next. I knew I would have to take care of my sister and keep us out of harm's way for another night. I wondered if we would have to put ourselves to bed again.

As I sat in there with my baby sister, I could hear him yelling, "I'm sick and tired of your accusations," and Mom weeping.

He beat her that night—tore open her shirt and left. She came to us, face wet and salty as she kissed ours and tucked us in for the night. This happened so often, that we were mechanized—we knew what to do and how to do it. Be quiet, stay hidden, and wait it out. This time she decided to stay with him. There were other times we hid in shelters or homes with other bruised children and eye-swollen mothers. I could still hear some Johnny Cash song skipping on the record player as my stepfather slammed the front door.

SHIT-KICKERS

NORMA

Sometimes Mom's personalities that were on view would cycle quicker than others. It may be months that my mother stayed within a certain alter while at other times she may have cycled quickly within a short period. This was one of those days.

I woke to go to school while my mother was at work. She often worked overnights to earn the extra money that came along with those shifts. So, getting myself off to school was not a new idea. I had just celebrated a birthday. I knew that after school my mother and I would be doing my actual birthday celebration as those things had to wait until payday and that day had come.

I got home after school and my mother was in a great mood. She asked me to get ready to go and as I was getting ready, she shifted to her flitting, flirting persona and put on extra makeup and did her hair. She sang in her sweet voice as she danced around getting ready to go out. We went out for dinner to a Chinese buffet, one of her favorite places because they had frog legs. We ate our dinner and small-talked about school and work. After dinner we went next door to the downtown pharmacy, and she giggled while she bought her favorite blond hair-dye and she convinced me to try the blue-black. I was sincerely enjoying myself. After our purchases she called a taxi to go to the mall. She said she had a surprise for me.

She was taking me to buy the buckskin cowboy boots I had been looking at for months. We entered the store and I tried the boots on, it wasn't the first time. She asked me in absolutes if I wanted them and would wear them. I was ecstatic. She slightly shifted again as she was laying out the money for the boots. She didn't appear angry or upset, just more adult. Like she took this seriously. I got it. I knew this was huge for us. I thanked her over and over and we stopped at the coffee shop that was situated in the corner of the mall. We both got chocolate raspberry. We sat at a table for two, in silence as we sipped our coffees and crunched on chocolate covered coffee beans. Then we walked home. As the walk went on my mother became quieter and quieter. I thought she was just tired.

It was a two mile walk home and she had worked all day (she never owned her own vehicle). Maybe that's what caused the shift, maybe it was the stress of spending the money, maybe it was none of that. Maybe it was something I'm still clueless about, but by the time we got home, she was angry. She said it was because I wasn't grateful, because I didn't understand what she went through to give me what I wanted. I was confused. I had repeatedly thanked her. I wasn't sure what else I was supposed to do. I didn't understand.

At the end of the night, those cowboy boots that I had wanted so badly were being held in her hands and used to hit me. She had grabbed onto the toes of the boots and used them like hammers. The heel of the boots hitting my head, my back, my body. I remember the smell of that new leather as it was shoved in my face. She couldn't properly hit me with them, they flopped around in her hands. She threw them at me, and I ducked as they hit the wall. She ran into the kitchen and I heard a sound I'll never get out of my head. The sound of metal scraping metal. My mother had grabbed a knife. She came back into the room and came at me with the knife. I didn't have much space to run, we were in such a tight place, but I knew I wasn't safe with my back against the wall. I stretched my arms out to my sides and was able to grab a broom.

At that moment I realized something I had never realized before. I was bigger than my mother. I had her by five inches. I had been working out at the local dojo. At that moment I dared do something I had never dared do. I fought back. I hit my mother with the broom, not hard. Just enough to stun her. I hit her arm and she dropped the knife and before she could react, I used the broom to push her up against the wall. I held the broom against her neck and pushed.

When she was still, I said to her, "If you ever put your fucking hands on me again, I will kill you." I meant every word of it. I hated myself for having wanted those boots so badly. The next day, I wore those boots proudly. I had earned them.

I can only assume the violent personalities were those of the ones who themselves had been abused. I like to believe that way because then it gives a reason for the brutal things we dealt with as children. She never did put her hands on me again after that day. But the mental and verbal abuse didn't stop until the day she died.

TRIGGERS
CELIA

Where we live, there are many gun owners—law enforcement, game hunters, and personal protection—and there is a great respect for military families, who also own firearms. Although a "military brat," I have long had an aversion to guns. I have oft heard members of my community tout that without people at the trigger, guns aren't killers. But fundamentally speaking, the only purpose of guns is to kill, whether justified because of residual hunter/gatherer experiences or for defense of country or offensive tactics in war. I have great respect for our military, which I must reiterate here. But my relationship with guns comes from a very different, dark place. As a child I learned very early that guns were used to control using fear, and I always understood that the main purpose of gun ownership was to either maim or to kill. I still have not ever held one, and probably never will.

BOOT CAMP
CELIA

Even now when I imagine confronting my stepfather to ask if he is sorry for any of it, my heart rate quickens and my breathing becomes erratic, which sounds much like a panic attack. I can usually talk myself out of a full-on panic attack, but it is exhausting. As a child, I was thin and sickly. Any time I did anything to displease him, there were various tortures he created just for me. Sometimes I received belt blows on the soft bottoms of my feet while I knelt on the hardwood floor. He also picked me up by my neck and throttled me, where neighbors surely heard and did nothing in the apartment next door.

I also remember being sent out to take the trash to the dumpster. The bag was heavy as I dragged it, and the dumpster was nearly a block away from our apartment. It was the dead of winter, so cold one couldn't touch metal with bare hands. I touched a metal post once and had to have hot water poured on my finger to remove it. One winter afternoon I was sent to do this chore and came upon two Doberman Pinchers, who charged me and knocked me on the ice. It was terrifying and although a dog-lover, I still avoid this breed.

In another instance, I was forced to kneel again, only this time, he took out his huge, white boots. My arms were thin. The boots were heavy. I had to keep my arms up, a boot in each hand, and if they touched the floor, I was whipped again with the belt. My arms burned and toes lost circulation. Our maternal grandmother used to say when hands or feet fell asleep that little birdies were fluttering around in there. If only that was true. I suppose those little birdies became part of a flight leitmotif of mine for years; consistently restless and travelling. Little did I know it started with these boots held up like pitiful offerings to a God I could not see and never heard.

HAPPY BIRTHDAY

NORMA

I had elf feet, which would have been funny if it weren't for the fact that they were also frozen. I had no shoes on and the dirtied wet socks that I was wearing curved upward and froze in the cold temperatures making my feet look like pointed little caricatures. I could not feel those curved toes anymore. I could not feel much anymore. I could barely see. I had been crying for hours as I hid from the world, hid from my mother, and hid from myself. I felt I could no longer go on anymore as I sat inside the frame of a tiny door on the bottom floor of the apartment building, I lived in with my mother. I was hidden well, between the dumpster and the building in the small back alley that the apartment building door opened into. I was a teenager, it was my birthday, and I was hiding outside in the snow. I was too afraid to go back home. There were so many thoughts running through my head. I would have to pass the storefront to get back inside to the foyer where our apartment door was located. I didn't want the patrons or the owners to see me. I didn't want to return home because I didn't know what would happen when I did. I was cold and I was hungry. The question was which of these thoughts weighed most heavily on my mind. In the end I chose warmth and headed back home.

As a teenager in the town that I grew up in there were many things that could have gotten me into trouble. I was not into drugs, I was not into drinking, and I had yet to discover boys. I found myself freezing outside on my birthday because I had gotten into trouble on my mother's terms. I had cut my thumb on the lid of a can while pushing the garbage down inside of the garbage can. A cut that maybe would have required a couple of stitches, if even that. Nothing too serious. I cleaned it up, put a bandage on it and forgot about it, until she came home. When my mother returned from her shifts at the hospital where she worked, she saw the blood and bandages in the garbage and asked me what had happened. I let her know that as I was pushing the garbage down into the bag a lid came up and cut me. Her eyes darkened as she looked at me. I knew what was coming next.

Her hand was like lightning and it came to my face with the determination of a boulder rolling down a hill. The blow came with such a sting and was accompanied by a darkness that spread over my eyes and was followed by a blinding sharp, white light. I looked down and tried to raise my hand to protect my face.

I begged her, "please don't, please!" but she just didn't listen. My fear and confusion took over as I knew I should not be getting hurt for having been hurt. Not everything my mother did made sense. I just knew that when she was mad, and I should shut up and take it; if I didn't the repercussions would get worse and worse. This time I did not heed my own warnings and I looked straight into her face and yelled, "Why are you doing this?"

Her response was what I expected. It was a dark blank stare as she pursed her lips and continued to hit. It seemed that I got that same answer for many of the things that I asked. I leaned back against the wall and my legs gave out from underneath me as I sank to the floor, crumpled into a ball, and sobbed. This was after all my birthday. I yelled louder.

"Why do you hate me so much? Why are you hurting me? What am I doing that's wrong? It's my birthday!"

She spun around looking at me with her dark, dark eyes and she leaned over, grabbed my shoulders, and put pressure on my neck as she whispered into my face.

"Shut the fuck up you filthy whore."

I jumped up and ran to the front door, forcefully opening it and ran as fast as I could down the stairs outside into the cold and found myself behind the building. There I hid for three hours in my T-shirt, shorts, and socks in the doorway of a rundown apartment building.

As I got colder and colder, I prayed for God to just let me slip into a quiet and peaceful sleep, but that sleep never came. Only the cold came over me. I knew she would not come looking for me. I knew that eventually I would have to go back home. So, as I walked through the snow, I kept my head down so that all the strangers wouldn't see the tears rolling down my face. I headed around to the front of my building, walked up a couple flights of stairs, and opened my front door. I went into my room and stripped the cold,

Beauty in Disrepair

wet clothing. I put on warm pajamas put a blanket over my shoulders and turned the small radio on that I kept in my room.

Just then my mother opened the door and walked in. I looked at her. I looked at her blue eyes; her stunningly blue eyes and she said to me, "Are you ready for dinner?" It was clear to me that: Nothing. Ever. Happened. As I sit here today, and I see the scar on my thumb from the day that I cut myself on the can I can remember everything just as if it were happening. In fact, that happens to me most days I glance at my body and some mark or some scar will remind me of something that happened when my life was so out of my hands.

It happens in a smell that I remember or a sound that is so familiar. Walking through Walmart I will hear a song and smell one's perfume and I'm gone, somewhere in a haze. Feeling a brush pulling too hard on the back of my head. Hearing a whisper of hate in my ear. It takes me back to those moments when I was helpless and alone. I don't normally go anywhere alone because these fears come rushing back every day. My past creeps up and grabs ahold of me like cold hands wrapped around my neck that will never let go.

When I see that scar on my thumb, I can still smell her breath as she would lean close to my face. I can still see her eyes so dark changing to the bright beautiful blue that they were. I can still hear the yelling and feel the embarrassment that maybe the neighbors who are upstairs could hear what I was going through. I can still feel the shame of living in a house like that. I flinch when someone moves by me too fast. My children must ask permission to hug me. They call this Post Traumatic Stress Disorder, PTSD.

ORDER IS SAFE
CELIA

Home and a sense of order or safety for me has been wherever I find myself most "grounded," which was never often. I think that when people meet me or get to know me, they think that I have it all figured out in life, but they mistake stability for order. As children, our physical space was always in flux, so now, everything in my life must have physical order. I only wish it were as easy to order my mind. As if the sense of obscured home was not enough, as a child, I always wondered why no one ever rescued us. Where were our saviors when Mom exploded into someone abusive? Where were they when she bit me and dug her long nails deep into the flesh of my arms? What about the bruises on my back or the constant profanities she hauled at me? The school nurse occasionally asked questions, but no action was ever pursued. Nothing was reported. The worst time of the year was summer because we did not have school to keep us safe for most of the day; we were either home alone or with Mom. Years later when she remarried my stepfather, she worked, and we were home *alone* with him. Summertime is supposed to be a time of life and happiness, warmth, and light. As a young child I loved the freedom of summers off but knew that the price I had to pay was more time alone with Mom. I suppose summertime is a trigger for me in that sense; I do know that I suffer depression and anxiety the most in these months.

I do not want to give the impression that only my sister and I suffered. As previously mentioned, Mom also was abused by my stepfather. I recall one time when Mom had sent my sister and I to the landlord's next door after a bad beating. I faintly remember knocking on the door with my little sister in hand, saying, "My Dad beat my Mom, and can you call the police?" This was not only a frightening situation as a child, but I knew even then that this was one of the worst beatings she had endured—so much so, that when police arrived, one of them vomited because of her puffed out eye, broken ribs, and other facial deformities. The landlord's family was kind enough to keep us overnight while we waited for

Mom's discharge from the local emergency room and shortly after, our uncle came to rescue us from harm's way as he always did. He always pulled us out of chaos and took us back to Gram's house, our place of safety and stability.

In another instance, my stepfather had beaten Mom and she took my sister and I to a women's shelter. The location was a remote town, isolated from larger towns and cities, like the ones we were stationed at for military service. One of the counselors came to our room and told Mom that she had a phone call. We went with her—Mom kept us close during those visits to shelters or kind neighbors. It was him on the phone. We could hear him pleading with Mom to come home with us, and even as a child, I knew that he was manipulating her. Her facial expressions and body flinches said it all. Her face became sympathetic, though, and the lines around her eyes and mouth softened. Then, we heard a gunshot tear through the phone receiver.

He had threatened to kill himself if we did not return immediately. When Mom sounded unsure, he shot off his gun and seconds later, we heard the kind of laughter that mocks, stings, and cuts. He had not shot himself at all, only shot off his service pistol. It was a sick way to convince her to come home, but it worked, and we ultimately returned. I knew the beatings would continue for all of us, and that he would probably make her have makeup sex while I watched my sister in the next room. Home is not always a place of safety and stability; it is often a place of chaos and fear for survivors.

PLAYTIME
CELIA

When Mom went to work and my stepfather was left alone with us, she often returned to find one of us children injured or terrified. One day she returned and found my lips swollen and my mouth bloody, as I sat in a heap in my bedroom. She confronted him and he seemed confused, as though he had no idea how it happened. But I knew. I told her. He had come into my closet, where I had set up a little playroom and tried some kind of martial arts kick on me. His foot connected with my face, hard, knocking me back and splitting my lip. I could taste metal on my tongue and felt the sting of swelling lips. As a schizophrenic he often didn't recall his angry tirades. He hid behind that mental illness, though, and when confronted, he either became more enraged (as with Mom) or scrambled to show affection. He put together an ice pack.

"We're just playing. We're friends," he smiled.

I remember the confusion in Mom's eyes as I sat on the kitchen counter, her dabbing the ice onto my swollen lips.

UNCERTAINTY

NORMA

We all have "telephone voice." That fake higher pitched us that we try to show initially to those incoming calls that we are unsure of. As the call goes on or as those calls are repeated, we usually and eventually slip back into our true voices, our true us. The thing with my mother is that life was always a game of "telephone voice." We didn't know what we were getting, when we were getting it, or for how long. As a child this unknown can be just as destructive as the alters themselves.

I didn't know who was waking me up or who I was coming home to. I didn't know whether to be happy or sedate. I was unsure of how quickly the switch would be made or if I would be the one to flip it. Stability is one of the most important influencers in a child's upbringing. We never had stable male influences. Men came and went often. Most of the relationships were abusive. I had found myself more than once clawing at the back of a man who had his hands wrapped around her neck. She found a couple of nice men, but they couldn't sign on for long; her alters were that destructive.

My mother switched from job to job, whether by choice I'm unsure. I never really thought anything of it when I was young. Her pay would increase and decrease. Her walk to work would increase and decrease. She would be doing so well at work and then get fired, sometimes she'd be doing fantastic and quit. I can only assume that if a child or violent alter had shown up while she was at work, not only would it cause a problem with her employers, but her confusion must have been overwhelming. Often personality changes are accompanied by periods of blackouts and the other personalities are unaware of what is going on. Yet, through all of this, she was always able to attain employment, assistance, or government help, which is how we survived year to year.

We were moved from school to school and apartment to apartment. By the time I graduated from high school I had attended seven schools. During high school alone we lived in four separate places. I was only in high school for three years. The most tumultuous time was during my middle school years, right after my sister had moved away and where I wasn't quite old enough to start defending myself. At one point during this time we lived above someone's garage. I had a woodstove and a radio. We were invited by the homeowners to use their bathroom, but for the most part my mother didn't want me to bother them, so I was forced to go outside in the woods to use the bathroom and washed with a pot of water that was on the stove.

We had lived in a church classroom for quite a few months one year. These changes made it impossible for the most part to keep friends. I couldn't have them over and could not go out with them. It wasn't until my freshman year of high school that I started expanding my circle and moving further away from home. I was realizing that things at my home were not normal. Something was wrong at my house. Something was wrong with my mother. I yearned for stability at that age and was lucky to find it with a small group of friends.

CLEANLINESS
NORMA

When things are bad, really bad it isn't unusual to hold on to glimpses of normality as one's savior. Something that can seem so mundane in the course of a day to most people can become a north star, guiding through a sea of chaos. A train with 600 boxcars or a secondhand cassette tape can see one through each day.

My mother had yet again just moved us. The apartment was supposed to be a one-bedroom, but that bedroom was only big enough to fit a twin mattress on the floor with no room to step around it. My mother slept on some discarded couch cushions pushed against each other with an old afghan blanket thrown on top against a wall in the living room. The only other furnishing in the living room was a radio/tape deck player on which we could get a few stations. The kitchen was big enough to hold the refrigerator, the sink and an upper and lower cabinet, there was no stove-top or oven. The bathroom was situated in the underneath of a staircase so if I stood too quickly off the toilet, I'd bang my head on the slanted ceiling. We had no phone, no cable, no paintings on the walls. The most decorative items in this home were the original hardwood floors and the checkerboard linoleum in the 4"x6" kitchen.

The apartment was ten yards from the railroad tracks. Those trains came and went twenty-four hours a day. At first the rattling and shaking of the trains kept me awake, but eventually the rocking put me to sleep or would slightly wake me in the night with its rhythmic music and then lull me back to sleep. There were two windows in the apartment and they both faced the tracks. They were my television. I watched the train pass and counted the cars. Most of the trains pulled their haul of 100 or 200 cars behind them, but that one time I had a half hour show as I watched her pull more than 600 cars of loot. When I got sick of watching this channel, I then studied the lyrics of a song as I listened over and over, as I did with "Stairway to Heaven."[1] I used these things to pass my time. The apartment

---

[1] Led Zeppelin. "Stairway to Heaven." *Led Zeppelin IV*. Perf. Jimmy Page. Atlantic Records, 1971.

so bare in its amenities and so bright without curtains, seemed so clean. Yet as I would learn here in this home, clean can be so dirty.

My mother handed me our last dollar and told me to go to the store around the corner and get a bar of soap. In our house dish soap usually doubled as shampoo, tripled as laundry detergent and was our home-made body wash, but soap was a special thing. I had been given the last dollar to get a bar of soap.

I got to the corner store and was pleasantly surprised that I had more than one option when it came to picking what soap I would bring home. There was a nice soap, but it smelled manly. I found the soap my grandmother used, which reminded me of her hugs. There was also a discounted, no-name brand that reminded me of mothballs. The third option was a no go. I went with the second because it made me happy and it was only 25 cents.

When I returned home and gave my mother the soap her reaction was unlike anything I had seen before. Her face wrinkled and became angry. She took the bar of soap and crumpled the box it was in.

She began screaming, "How could you do this to me?" I was so confused. "This isn't deodorant soap!"

I didn't know there was a difference. There are soaps that clean and soaps that clean and deodorize. She began violently slamming the bar of soap into her groin, screaming and growling as she did so. I screamed at her to stop.

"You've wasted our money on this shit, now I'll smell like pussy!"

I've replayed this scene in my mind repeatedly, especially when I smell the soap I picked. It took me years to tell my husband to stop buying it. I'm unsure if the person who was so angry at me that day was over-sexualizing the situation, or if perhaps it was one of her male alters upset at the possibility of smelling like a female.

Beauty in Disrepair

HYPOCHONDRIA
CELIA

Mom was mentally and physically ill; we always knew that much, even if we didn't know what to call it as children. However, her mental illness was far worse than any of the physical disorders in which she may have suffered. In reviewing old doctor notes and hospital invoices, it is clear that she had cancer at one time, and had it removed from her jaw and breasts. She later had more lumps in her breasts, which were benign. Still, she told us she may not come home after these hospital stays—that she may in fact, die. We had so many scares like this as children, that eventually, we stopped believing she was ill at all. Further complicating her illnesses, was her unnatural ability to morph into someone else. She was able to attain a college degree and was so smart, that she probably applied many of her supposed illnesses or afflictions from her studies. If a disease was mentioned in casual conversation, she was sure to weigh in or compare it to her much worse illness(es).

I recall lengthy letters sent to my teachers or placed right on the back of my report cards—all excuses as to why I was absent, or my grades were slipping. I missed a lot of school as a sickly child, but often, Mom somehow made our illnesses her own. We later learned that she also had Munchhausen by Proxy: we were always in/out of doctor's offices or emergency rooms as children. She absorbed every bit of pity or attention it brought. Yes, we had illnesses, but these were often exacerbated by the stress and strain of constantly moving, not having enough to eat, and physical abuse. We missed a lot of school but were still expected to maintain A's in everything and when I did not (my sister aced everything easily), we suffered the consequences.

SICK
NORMA

I crawled into bed one night when I was a pre-teen and as I lay there, I felt discomfort in my chest. I was a young girl and had just gone out to buy my first training bra. I thought the discomfort was related. After a few weeks, the discomfort turned to pain. At this time, I went to my mother to explain to her what I was feeling. After she had asked me a few questions and felt around where I was feeling the pain, she found that I had a few masses in the area of the lymph nodes that I had on my right shoulder, neck, arm and breast. My mother brought me to the hospital that night. After being examined in the emergency room I was sent up to the surgical floor to await a biopsy in the morning. The doctors feared because of my mother's cancer history that this may be the same. The next day the biopsy was completed, and the results came back as lymph reticulosis, also known as Cat Scratch Fever; an infection carried in many felines that can be transmitted through open wounds. Particularly a kitten's scratch. The infection and surrounding lymph nodes were taken out and I was put on antibiotics and sent home to heal. Something in my mother changed at this time. I believe she realized the sicker I was the more attention she received.

What should have been an easy healing process at home turned into a drawn-out painful experience. Anybody who's had surgery before knows that sometimes the worst part of it can be the removing of the bandages and tape that come along with wound care. My mother changed the bandage over my shoulder every hour. By the fourth or fifth change the pain was pretty intense. At this time, she got her downstairs neighbor to hold my legs still so she could pull the tape off and re-apply the bandage consistently every hour or two, for two or three days. On the third day the pain was so much, and the skin was so raw that she had to return me to the hospital. I had developed an infection surrounding the surgical site because of the antagonizing way she treated it. I was given more antibiotics and sent home once again to recover. Two days later my mother had me put my kitten on a leash and walk it to the pound so that it could be put down. She told me that this was my punishment for letting it make me sick.

Through this experience people helped my mother, they brought over food and gifts and lent her an ear more than ever. Over time my mother learned tricks which would help garner more attention from neighbors, co-workers, and church goers. She learned of a floral allergy I had and added perfumes to my bathwater containing the allergen to cause rashes and reactions that needed to be attended to. She withheld medicines when I was fevered and used herbal tinctures to produce immune responses. I particularly recall months at a time when I was told to consume pint after pint of Hibiscus flower tea which can cause toxic reactions in the body including hallucinations and infertility. I was also given large amounts of Rosehips which can cause kidney problems.

These were just a few of the issues I faced along with many episodes of food poisoning and constant stress. It was only in my early twenties that all of this culminated in the knowledge that my mother must have also suffered with a mental illness called Munchausen's by Proxy. In short, she made me sick to reap the benefits of attention. At nineteen, my gallbladder had to be removed because of what my doctor called "starvation syndrome." As he explained it, because I had gone without eating so much as a child by the time I had been on my own for a while and was consuming a normal diet my gallbladder went into shock. It did not know how to process fats and proteins. By the time I was in my twenties I was legally classified as disabled because of a host of illnesses and auto-immune disorders including Fibromyalgia, chronic kidney problems, seizures and more. To date I take over twenty medications daily. Although I cannot attribute all of this to my mother's behavior, I do believe it is a contributing factor to my health and physical well-being. She taught my body how to attack itself.

There were other instances of my mother trying to use my health to gain admiration or attention. Any health problems I was having though were discussed with friends, preachers, or co-workers. I hardly ever saw a doctor and I know now that this was to hide the things that she was doing to my body.

In my teens, after one particularly fearsome migraine, my

mother did finally bring me to a neurologist because our pastor suggested it. After examining me, he asked my mother to leave the room while he asked some personal questions. To this day I don't know what I said that gave it away, but he knew. He called it quicker than anyone else ever had in my life. He called her out on it. He suggested that maybe some of her behaviors were contributing to my stress, adding to my headaches, and making things harder for me as I was just a child.

She reared up like a cornered lion. I'd never seen her charge at someone before. It was like she was guarding her prey, me. They yelled back and forth. He promised to call the authorities; she swore she'd take his medical license. This went on for about five minutes while I cried in the background. I cried because I knew what was coming when I got home. And I was right.

The beating was frantic. She clawed, hit, and kicked every chance she got. I curled up into a ball on the floor to try to wait out the anger's storm. This storm seemed to go on forever. When she was done, I laid on the floor; coughing, sobbing, and drooling into the acrylic smell of the cheap carpet on our floor. My eyes almost swollen shut pictured the fibers on the floor as little swirls of brown that were swaying underneath the weight of my tears. I laid there and cried myself to sleep.

That same year I came down with the chicken pox. As we age chicken pox become more aggressive. I had it as a teenager and it was a pretty rough case. They were under my eyelids, in my vagina and created open sores in the webbing between my fingers and toes. She waited until the disease had accessed my lungs to bring me to the hospital. It took many weeks for me to begin to feel better.

OXYGEN SUPPLY
CELIA

I recall I had grown increasingly sickly because of the breathing problems. I could not run like other kids anymore—stairs were even a challenge. Mom knew I needed more medicine, so all four of us set out to go to the local drug store. My stepfather was angry at the inconvenience. That was her job, but she did not drive and needed a ride. He always drove; he was always in control. She became angry with him and they argued. As we pulled into the parking lot, she got out of the car and slammed the door. He immediately sped off. As I looked through the rear window at my mom watching us leave in angst, my baby sister began to wail. She realized we were leaving Mom behind. What happened next was so fast that I only recall snips of visuals. In those days, no one wore seatbelts. He reached behind the seat, grabbed her by the back of the neck, and slammed her little head into the floor. I sat motionless, not understanding why he did it or what I should do.

She stopped crying immediately and looked up so stunned, that we were both frozen. She was probably in shock. I am sure I held her still to avoid further abuse, but what I will never forget is that look on her little face. She suffered from seizures periodically after that incident. In addition, later that night when Mom came home after having to hike for miles, she administered my medicine as I lay in bed, my sister already sleeping. She was crying and had brush bristle marks up and down her arms, an abuse she would years later inflict on me. She was shaking but she was home. I fell into a drug-induced, restless sleep.

ALTERS AT ODDS
NORMA

I could see the panic in her face. My mother had such beautiful blue eyes, but when this panic showed itself, they would change to a blue steely gray color, dilated and searching.

"Put your fingers down your throat and gag yourself!" She was screaming at me.

I didn't know how to do it. I was only a child; I had never made myself throw up. Her screams became more exasperated and her movements jerking. I had my arms flung around the porcelain bowl holding on for dear life, my legs wrapped around the base of the toilet cooling my thighs underneath my flannel nightgown. My long, brown hair was curled around her fingers and she tossed my head back and forth screaming at me to vomit. I held steadfast to the toilet as my head was tossed from one direction to the next.

"We're going to die! We've been poisoned! Get it out!"

She shoved her fingers down my throat. I choked and gagged, but nothing happened. I started to cry as her fingers buried themselves tighter in my hair pulling my head backwards. Her panicked face so close to mine. Frantic and confused her eyes darted around the room, back at me and suspiciously took in our surroundings. Her face was so close to mine and I could smell the acrid bile on her lips. I was terrified for her. I was made to be terrified for her. Now I was terrified for me. The empty and bloated can of clam chowder we had eaten for dinner a couple hours earlier sat in the garbage now. She had purged what she had eaten and was trying to get me to do so.

It wasn't until many years later that I understood. One of her alters had fed us; one of her alters had found the can.

Chapter 2
RELIGION AND FAITH IN DISREPAIR

HALLELUJAH
CELIA

Are you God, in your robes and sashes …
the one who gives us manna?
Selah.
Do you bless the wine and sprinkle us
with holy water?
Amen.
Frankincense seeps under the pews—do you
hypnotize?
Peace be with you.
If you're God, will you see me reach into Gram's
purse for candies?
And also with you.
Will you see me eye the offering basket, hungry?
Or will you close your eyes?

I BELIEVE

NORMA

One aspect of my mother's disease that I've benefited from was the distinctive changes between beliefs and religions. One year we'd be strict Southern Baptists studying the Bible from front to back and living accordingly. Singing Hymns every Sunday and Wednesday and attending every Bible study they offered. The next we'd be burning sage and drumming to call on Native American ancestors to free us from the curses of "the white man." She told stories of the "old ways" and her meeker self was usually present.

We were Pentecostal for a time. She lay her hands on the members of the church to promote their healing. I had to attend classes to learn how to be a lady and my child self was trying for the life of me to learn how to speak in other tongues, a supposed secret prayer language. I never figured it out. When my mother was Wiccan, I learned the ways of the Earth. She taught me how to spot chamomile for tea, and plantain leaves for healing properties. For my mother, things seemed to come back in three's.

I learned the Bible, herbs, and spices, and read from the Torah. We ate crackers during Passover and fish during Lent. I took Communion on Sundays and burned oils for protection. And all of this as confusing as it was, I'm glad I did. For if not for the faith I have, which was provided to me by every belief that I had seen, I may have not survived the things that I have gone through. I pull from all faiths of the world now to teach my children and to guide myself. I still pray to a God I know must be there. There is beauty in disrepair.

SACRED SPACE
CELIA

Mom changed religions almost as often as she shifted alters. She practiced everything from fundamental Christianity to a form of Wicca. As such, we church-hopped from Catholic, Southern Baptist, Pentecostal, and Native American beliefs. My sister and I were expected to believe as whole-heartedly as she did—at that time in that belief system. Subsequently, as in her more severe, abusive personalities or alters, her faith-based system became more cultish as she rigidly forced religious dogma down our throats. Coupled with what some religious leaders enforced, we were involved in a Holy War against homosexuals, those unsaved by "the blood of Jesus," or those who did not adhere to strict, apocalyptic tirades. I became completely disenfranchised by all organized religion. Like my sister, I do have respect for any of those which I've mentioned. However, I no longer believe in organized religion for myself; I find the collective lack of tolerance in others as sinful as sin itself—what's more, it is hypocrisy. I do not believe I will ever again be able fully to be a part of a religious system—if none of those accept people from all walks of life. I do, however, believe in a God—although I am unsure of the form or gender of that entity.

Ultimately, I have never quite felt as though I belonged in mainstream society; as such, those who were born different physically, sexually, or psychologically have often felt like an extended family for me. I cannot imagine that God loves them any less; nor do I value my life or beliefs more than theirs. If only we could all know that we are truly loved, regardless of the decisions we make or the beliefs we ascribe to, and that we are all God's children and this will ultimately see us through our most difficult times. I am thankful that I own my identity and beliefs now; how awful for Mom to lose her own amidst the voices in her head.

SPEAKING IN TONGUES
CELIA

After reading the first two examples, readers may wonder if there were there any instances of good that came out of our religious and supernatural experiences. Yes. We often found patience, understanding, and comfort; a sense of family that we missed during years that Mom kept us from our own. However, in the more fundamentalist, evangelical churches, although my sister and I benefited from the church school environment to allay our social fears and personal anxieties, for we were both introverted, we also suffered some strange interactions. Fundamentalism is extremely rigid in its portrayal of Christianity and the King James version of the Christian Bible. Scriptures are often taken out of context, religious text are analyzed very literally, which is true of many belief systems, but some churches believed in speaking in tongues. I faked it so I wouldn't be thought of as less holy. I am not saying that it doesn't work, but it never worked for me. It became a popularity contest—who could worship best, dance the hardest, or speak in a prayer language. It was all a distortion that led to legalism in and spiritualism that was overbearing and often contrived by hypocrites who worshipped on Sunday because they partied on Saturday.

There were healers and prophets. Some were authentic; some were not. There were certain men in the church who hugged us teenage girls a little too closely, laid hands on us during prayer a little too often, and who prophesized to invoke their own interpretations of God's messages. Mom bought into all of it just like she had in other religions. Repeatedly, members were asked to confess before God and the congregation—but I thought that only God needed to hear our confessions, unlike within the Catholic church, where there were confessionals with priests to hear our sins. I still fear that kind of psychological and sometimes physical control from other religious organizations and so I still do not belong to any church and have not since I left that one. I will visit churches, take photographs of cathedrals around the world, and pray on my own. But I will say again, I will never belong to one.

It wasn't all bad, though. There was music. Thank God for the music, as it was my only spiritual connection to God within the church. Music was and always will be my prayer language. I came out of my shell when I sang or played piano, and I am grateful for that time in my life, because it has helped me to heal. Music has helped me to cope, to escape, and to recognize that there can be beauty in disrepair.

A WITCH
CELIA

Mom often thought the world was out to get us. One of her most paranoid times was when she thought I turned the church against her. One instance that exemplifies exactly what Mom did to show how un-Christian I was took place in a pastor's office. Mom had called a meeting because I was hard to control—she thought I was a rebellious teenager (a label my father would eventually give to me). She thought I had forsaken God and was exhibiting demonic behaviors. What was her proof? She held before him several drawings I had doodled. Her interpretation of those mindless sketches was false. Not only was I not an artist, as my sister, but also, I had no ulterior motives or messages within those doodles other than sheer boredom. In fact, the pastor waited a beat before he looked at me, then Mom.

He said something like, "Ah … I'm not sure what you are seeing here, but I find no evidence of evil or negativity."

Mom did not respond well to this. She feigned acceptance but of course, I knew that when we got home I would either be bitched at or beaten for embarrassing her. She maintained that I had turned the church people against her. She even went as far as to say that someone in the church had called her a witch because of the mole on her nose. Then it was ridiculous and embarrassing for us kids, but now, I can see some humor in it, albeit a cliché depiction of a witch. I suppose my dark sense of humor was born in some ways out of the ridiculous, the inflamed, the uber-collective ideology that contrives that one believer is right and one is wrong. Why can't we be both? Why can't we be comfortable in the liminal spaces and not fixated by absolutes. We floated in and out of absolutes all our lives—we just didn't know who or what would bring them about in our mother and her shifting beliefs.

THE ZEALOT
NORMA

It was a Saturday and I awoke to the flu and miserable cramps. I just wanted to melt into my pillow and waste away my weekend. I lay on my twin mattress that sunk into the floor and stared at the empty white ceiling. My mother let out a yelp and hollered for me. I struggled up off the floor and rushed to her yells. She was in the bathroom of the small apartment we lived in. This place we called home was barely bigger than a fancy walk-in closet, but was a step up from the week by week hotel we had been staying in. The apartment was a hallway that turned onto itself with a bathroom no bigger than a port-a-potty. We had to wash in the bathroom sink. It was here that I found my mother pointing to something under the bathroom sink. It was a mouse stuck to a live sticky trap. A cruel trap that held the mouse so that if it tried to escape its fur would be ripped off, skin attached. She was screaming for me to take it out to the dumpster behind the building.

Again, I had the flu, cramps and it was not even 8:00 a.m. I rolled my eyes. Unfortunately, not out of her sight and because I wasn't feeling well, I didn't move fast enough. She was able to hit the back of my head with her open hand and screamed for me to take the mouse out to the garbage. I felt horrible, both physically and emotionally. I hated hurting anything, even this small mouse. I didn't want to put the poor live thing into the garbage to die a slow and painful death. What a great way to start the day. Little did I know it was only going to go downhill from here. Tumbling, rolling, and screaming downhill.

I walked downstairs and outside, opened the lid to the garbage can placed the mouse inside, cried and put the lid back on. After the tears stopped, I walked back upstairs went inside and crawled back into bed. I rolled to face the wall and cried myself back to sleep, but that was short-lived.

A high pitched and joyous scream woke me from my sleep. I rolled onto my back and then I heard his voice. The Zealot was back.

My mother peeked her head around the corner of the wall and threw a pack in my direction, "Pack for a couple days."

Beauty in Disrepair ~ 43 ~

"Where are we going?" I asked.

"Camping," she said.

"Mom, I'm sick and I have my period." The tears were coming. Oh God, I knew I couldn't hold them back. She came to the bed and leaned as low as she could.

"Pack the fucking bag and don't ruin this for me."

I got up and packed my bag. Of course, this was something that I learned at a very young age. Never, NEVER, get in between my mother and any man she may be with, in life or in her head. Before we left, I made my bed, fed the cat, and put out some extra water out for him and went out to check the mail. In the mailbox was a card from my sister; ten dollars and a note. I quietly slipped it into my pack and let my mother know I was ready to go.

By 10 a.m. we were headed out of town to go hiking and camping. I was in the back of his Van: a living, breathing paradox of Christianity and sin. Gospel tracts and New Testament Bibles were strewn about the shag carpeting along with psychedelic music and empty beer bottles. Cramps, motion sickness and the smell of rancid beer enveloped me, and I dropped into the faux leather bench and fell asleep.

I awoke sometime later, and we had not yet reached our destination. I don't know if we even had one, I just know that at that time we were still winding through some back roads through this rural scenery. I asked if there was somewhere we could stop so I could use the bathroom. My belly was upset, and I knew that I needed to take care of my personal hygiene. The Zealot refused, telling me that we would arrive at his friends' home in the woods shortly.

"Where are we going?" I asked. I had thought we were headed to a specific town.

"Don't question me!" He shouted.

I was confused. I had just wanted to know where we were going. He and my mother went back to giggling and smiling with their hands on each other's thighs; talking of God and singing along to his eight track tapes of Three Dog Night. We kept driving for quite some time and I was becoming very uncomfortable. I asked once again if I could stop and use the bathroom. I let the Zealot know that I would even be willing to go in the woods on the side of the road. He replied with a stern look and let me know that we would be arriving at his friend's house where we would eat and rest. That gave me a sort of reassurance and so I crossed my legs and hoped for the best.

After another while we pulled up to a shabby A-frame house nestled into the woods in the middle of a small county. My mother and he got out of the car. I moved up to open the door and realized there was no handle to get out.

He looked at me and said, "a child of God would not be so disrespectful to her parents. I think you should just stay here and think about what you've done." He slammed the door and locked it from the outside with some kind of padlock. My mother mouthed the words "I'm sorry," and shut her door. Again, I saw that there was no way to open that door from the inside. I was trapped. I was in the back of a van in the middle of nowhere, hungry, and tired. I did not know if the people inside even knew if I was out there. What bothered me most was that I still had to pee.

The sun started to set, and shadows moved into the trees. The lights in the A-frame house came on one by one. I could see through the glass windows as everyone sat at the kitchen table eating, talking and laughing and I began to cry, softly at first and then harder and harder and then I couldn't hold it anymore and my bladder let loose. I squatted on the floor of the van so I wouldn't get the bench I was sleeping on wet. The blood tinged urine worked its way through the shag carpeting and pooled on the burnt orange carpet by a stack of Bibles in the back of the van.

I'm not sure what time it was when I was woken up. I do know that it was pitch black outside. The deep woods blocked any stars that may have been out that night. The Zealot popped his head inside the door and asked,

"Are you ready to apologize?"

"For what?" I asked.

"Spoiled, ungodly child!" he screamed and slammed the door. I was alone again. I tested the doors again. I squatted on the floor again and then laid down to sleep once again.

A tie-dye and jean shorts. That is what I had put on the day before for our "hiking and camping" trip. This morning they were covered in piss, blood, and sweat. My face was swollen from crying and my hair matted with tears. I had to peal the hair from my face to get it out of my eyes. The sun had only been up for a couple of hours, but the van was acting like an oven and I was getting hotter and hotter. I was so thirsty and the stench inside the cage was making me nauseous.

I saw my mom leave the A-frame and head towards me, she opened the door and told me to grab my bag so that I could shower. I walked into the stranger's house reeking and stained and was shown their bathroom. I let the water run down my tired body for a very long time, got dressed and was returned to the van. I had gotten through a good portion of the New Testament when they returned to the van and said we were going on a hike. I don't remember where or how long it took to get there. I tried to sleep as much as I could. I was so hungry, thirsty, and tired. Then I had to climb a mountain.

It was cool out, not cold, but in the shade of the trees the temperature couldn't have been more than 50 degrees, but I was bundled in sweat clothes. The climb started over exposed tree roots and overgrown ferns. It had been raining off and on for the last week or so and mud lay over the trail which hadn't yet been cleared of debris from the no doubt menacing storms it had been fighting through the season. But it was beautiful. The temperature was beginning to climb and I had yet to eat or drink in about 48 hours, all I could think of was how my tongue was sticking to the roof of my mouth, feeling every taste bud swollen with the expectation of some sort of gratification. My top lip was sticking to my teeth, so I began thinking of lemons to make my mouth water. They walked in front of me without a care in the world, as if I weren't there, lost in a world I wanted no part of.

The hike started to intensify, as our elevation increased it became less of a stroll and more of workout as I had to hold on to rocks and roots to make my way up the summit. Two hours after beginning we took the top of the mountain where at the top a fire tower and pockets of blueberry shrubs waited for us. Blueberries.

I was so excited to see those plants. I went to a crop of bushes sat on the ground and started picking the ripe berries and placing them in my shirt that I had turned up to make a soft cradle to hold them. The Zealot and my Mother were doing their thing, so I paid no mind. Twenty minutes into picking and eating my Mother called for me; asking me to join them. As I walked towards them, I could see the anger in his face. I knew I had done something wrong; I just didn't know what. I sat next to them, ready to flinch.

"Why so greedy?" He said.

I was puzzled, "Greedy about what?" I asked.

The Zealot put his hand on my shoulder, "Well, I've had the decency to let you stay in my car. I've brought you to this place and to the top of this mountain, why would you eat without giving that to me?"

I couldn't believe he was serious. He was and my mother; her expression was one of condescension and pity. I lifted the apron I had made of my shirt and poured the remainder of my berries into his hands. When he was done eating, we began down the mountain.

The trip down seemed almost ominous, like I knew when we got to the bottom there was something to fear. As if the mountain was screaming *Wait until your father gets home!* I tried to get ahead of them on the trail, I just let gravity pull my legs over the leaves, over the roots, not caring if one grabbed my foot and pulled me into its bony arms. I just wanted to tumble and roll down the great hill as far away as I could. They wouldn't let me, every few minutes I would hear, "You better not get out of our sight!" So, I would slow and let them catch up and then once again start running.

I was right though; the trip was only meant to get worse. We arrived back to his van and got inside. I seemed to be the only one aware of the smell inside, or maybe I was the only one who cared. He began the drive to Saranac Lake as he and my mother sang along to the radio. At dusk we pulled up alongside a bridge. It was beautiful. A stone bridge in the woods a few stories above thrashing and rolling water snaking over the jagged rocks below. It was a picturesque scene. He looked at my mom.

"Stay in the car." Then he turned and looked at me. The Zealot walked around to my door and opened it, "get out," he droned. His face was stern but there was a smile behind his eyes.

Beauty in Disrepair

"Mom?" It was more of a pleading than a question. She didn't even turn her head to look at me. I got out of the van and faced down-stream, watching the white caps wash over the stones below. In an instant his hand was around the back of my neck squeezing hard. I was being pushed forward and I clung to the stone wall that was the barrier between the road and the river.

"Repent!" he yelled. I began to cry. "Repent for your sins!" he bellowed. I knew I wasn't guilty of crimes against God. The Zealot wanted me to beg for his forgiveness. He wanted to pardon me. I could barely get the words out to ask him why as I was so frightened and short of breath. He pulled a pocketknife from his belt and slowly opened it with his other hand, slowly turning it back and forth as if memorized by it or what it could do.

"Repent or face death." His squeeze was getting harder. I did the only thing I knew to do, and I began to pray.

I recalled a few lines from a scripture: "Our Father who art in Heaven, Hallowed be Thy Name ... ".[2] As I continued with my prayer the Zealot seemed to calm and slowly his grip on me loosened. I was put back in the van and we continued the journey through the mountains.

We arrived in the next town that night by which time my hunger was eating away at me. Rounding around the corner by a fast food restaurant I remembered that I had slipped the note my sister sent me into my bag at the start of the trip. I excitedly asked my Mother if we could stop, so I could get something to eat as my sister had given me ten dollars. She said yes and they pulled the van into the parking lot. I was almost shaking with excitement as I ran inside, used the bathroom, and then stood in line for a chicken sandwich, French fries, and cola. When I got the bag of hot food it smelled so good. Little things seem so big when they are all you have. I pushed my way out the door and into the parking lot where my mother was standing outside the van.

"He's very upset you didn't offer to buy him anything," she said.

"But I only had ten dollars, Mom," I countered.

---

[2] *The Holy Bible: King James Version.* Matthew 6:9-13. Bible Gateway, www.biblegateway.com. Accessed 20 Jul. 2020.

Again, she let me know how upset he was and opened the van door. I stepped inside and he held out his hand. I wondered as he ate if it tasted as good as it smelled. In the background the lyrics wormed through my head as they came out of the eight-track player. "One is the Loneliest Number."[3]

---

[3] Nilsson, Harry. "One." *Three Dog Night*. Dunhill Records, 1968.

POSSESSED
CELIA

There was another instance of Mom's paranoia or possibly, a connection with evil. We lived on a street that had a lot of pedestrian traffic, so I'm not sure how only Mom saw this "being" she described to us. She described a man—or something like a man—walking toward her, head forward and body stiff. He was all in black and when he got closer to her, she said he only had whites for eyes. He walked briskly past her and she later recounted the tale to us, although we were children and surely would have nightmares. I do believe that there is good and evil in this world, but I doubt my mother's ability to really "see it." Perhaps it was an extension of one of her alters? Her abuser from childhood? It is difficult today to know if what she saw was real, given what we now know about Dissociative Identity Disorder. Maybe one of her personalities conjured this image, or maybe this really was something from the other side—an omen—or a reflection of her own demonic possession. It is hard to know what possession was and what was psychological. I have spent my life trying to reconcile the sometimes-unexplainable events of my childhood, and I believe that I have concluded that Mom suffered both from DID and at times, the influences of forces intangible in our natural world.

For example, when Mom was near the end of her life, I called in a priest to do last rites. I later sat with her in the hospital room. She was in and out of consciousness, and I do not know if she was really "there" with me or somewhere between here and the beyond—as though she had begun that journey to the other side but was transfixed in the natural world. She became visibly agitated and stared straight ahead at the privacy curtain, and as she watched shadow movements under it, she seemed to be caught in a horrific trance. She was terrified, and I tried to call her back, begging her to look away and to focus on me instead. As she slowly turned her head toward me, she stared and what happened next, I still cannot explain with an educated, rational answer.

Maybe I saw something that was the result of my own exhaustion of staying up late, awaiting her condition to turn, even though it was grim. Her gall bladder erupted, and she was in full sepsis. Maybe I was anticipating her death and was afraid of what she was seeing or where she would end up. Maybe what I saw was real. I did not want to infer that mental illness was wrapped up in demonic possession or vice versa, given the history of how society previously viewed mental illness. But as she turned her head and fixed her gaze on me, she did not seem to recognize who I was as her eyes turned completely black. It felt and looked so real that I asked my sister to call a family friend, a former pastor of ours, to come and pray over her in addition to the last rites she was given.

A storm had brewed very quickly that night, and the pastor and his daughter almost did not make it to the hospital. It all seemed so surreal, like something was keeping them away and she and I separate from them. When they finally arrived, they prayed over her and I had seen this pastor deal with demonic possession before, so it gave some comfort. Whether it worked to free her or not, her eyes never changed again, and I believe that she was free when she died. Although some may find my actions morbid, I have always been drawn to eyes, and hers were no exception. I had her eyes. Before her body was moved for preparation, I had to make sure that her eyes were hers again—a lovely blue, as I gently lifted an eyelid to see. To my great relief, I saw her baby blues.

Chapter 3
SEXUALITY IN DISREPAIR

I KEEP THE LIGHT ON
CELIA

Often when I can't sleep I keep the light on.
In the dark I fear
the hands that grope,
the fiendish face that fondles—
I fear.
I fear, fear.
I lay there—Mom sleeping
down the hall—
in the dark
he comes.
He *comes.*
I pretend to sleep,
breathing heavily.
What a good little actress.

"Good girl! Tomorrow you get a toy. We'll see."

I'm always tired.
Night terrors.
He is sprawled across the couch,
sleeping.
I put myself to bed with
my baby sister.
Such a good girl.

I still sometimes fall asleep with the light on,
when I do sleep.

Beauty in Disrepair

HIS POWER
CELIA

I closed my eyes and saw the darkness reaching:
I held my breath, relieved he'd stopped the fight.
I rocked my body—uncovered, cold, bleeding.

Mom crouched with shaking hands stretched, pleading.
Her fear had been confirmed; she had been right.
I closed my eyes and saw the darkness reaching.

Opening his fist: "You deserved that beating."
Now catatonic, he turned on the light.
I rocked my body—uncovered, cold, bleeding.

I knew so little then what was worth keeping.
Mom stood, trembling. "He had no right!"
I closed my eyes and saw the darkness reaching.

His eyes were glazed, his mouth, gaping—
the angry words, the hostile grope of night.
I rocked my body, uncovered, cold—bleeding.

She rocked me, shaking—tears softly breaching
the gap in me: the shame, the fear, the night.
I closed my eyes—saw the darkness reaching.
I rocked my body: covered, cold, bleeding.

COME TO ME
CELIA

My sister was only a toddler when we were stationed back home at the end of my stepfather's military service. I have had Asthma since birth, and it was much worse as a child than as an adult. I was allergic to many foods, environmental elements, and seasonal changes in temperature caused serious breathing issues. I am sure the stress of the household contributed to my breathing struggles in the night. Or was there something else that led to those late-night asthma attacks, when Mom brought my inhaler, propped my pillows, and tried to lull me to sleep? One night I recall waking because I felt something on my face. I rubbed my sleepy eyes and when I opened them, I saw my stepfather standing above me, erect penis in hand. Mom came into view in the doorway, flipped on the lights, and saw him standing over me, completely naked.

I cannot recall anything else about that night except him leaving the room, Mom coming in with a wet washcloth to wipe my face clean. White, crusty flakes fell from my face, as she tearfully cleaned me. I later came to understand that he had ejaculated on my face. If anything, else occurred that night, I have blocked it completely. I do not know if he fondled and/or raped me that night or any other time, but I do recall that I barely bled during my first sexual encounter. At times during sexual intercourse or sexual acts of any kind, I become completely frozen or disconnected. That memory will come out when I am ready to handle it; until then, it remains lodged somewhere, a dormant but horrifying recollection.

My view of men in general was jaded and I was a late bloomer regarding sexuality. Even before I became sexually active, Mom constantly referred to some men as *whoremasters* and me, a whore. Her accusations always confused me. I suppose in many ways, I have always confused sex with making love. I have often thought of it as dirty, sinful, and sometimes, painful. I know now lacking positive male role models skewed my view of male/female relationships. I wish I had positive male role model in those early years of adolescence to guide me and to help me understand that not all men are monsters.

I did have some examples of that in my later teens, as my friends' families welcomed me to stay for brief periods in their homes. There I learned how teenagers can talk to their parents about sex—even ask questions. Thinking back on this, I know my mother did not mean to call me a whore or worse, and that it was one of her alters talking, but the words stung, and the shame prickled throughout my body. I still struggle with my own sense of sexuality and am unable to perform certain acts of intimacy. I have fluctuated between promiscuity and prudishness much of my adult life. Now, I am finally in a place in which I call the shots; I do things on my terms, not anyone else's. There is still much guilt associated with sex, but I have learned to be patient and to accept only what I can handle and deny what doesn't feel right or safe for me.

DIRTY GIRL
NORMA

Oversexualization was something I dealt with many times growing up. Innocent situations could be turned into elongated stories of perversion. At night I would be tucked into bed with my arms outside my blankets. It wasn't unlikely for me to be woken up with a backhand to the face for having worked my hands under the blanket while I slept. Her fear was that I would be masturbating and that was unacceptable.

I physically matured quickly during puberty. By the time I was a freshman in high school my chest was enormous! My friends lovingly nick-named me "Double-D." One day as my mother and I were walking down the street, a friend of mine was passing by and yelled, "What up Double- D?" I waved and my mother's hand went to the back of my neck. Her nails dug in and she walked me like that the rest of the way home. Tears ran down my face, as I knew what I was in for when I got home. I stayed home from school the next day, mostly to conceal my embarrassment from what I know my friend saw. The bruises were only secondary.

I was always reprimanded about using the bathroom with a female friend because it was an act of perversion. I just thought all the girls went to the bathroom in pairs.

During one walk home during middle school, my mother was telling me some news that wasn't great. I turned to her and said, "That really sucks!" Her face went from conveying a casual look to darkening in a split second. The changes were stunning. Artwork. Like lenticular pictures that had grooves so when I viewed them from different angles the picture would change. The picture would change but never the source.

She said very quietly, "Just wait until we get home."

I was eleven or twelve at the time and I already knew to fear what that meant. We were only 100 feet from home. I didn't have enough time to prepare. I didn't know what to be sorry for. I wasn't sure why I was so scared. We got inside our apartment and as soon as the door closed her hand closed around my wrist and she pulled me close to her. Our faces barely inches apart. the acrid stench of old coffee and cigarette smoke coming from her mouth as she breathed her fire on me.

"Who the fuck do you think you are?" I'm sure my confusion shown on my face. "Do you even know what that means?"

I spun the question around in my head quickly. I replied, "Doesn't it mean something is bad?"

"No! It means you're sucking on a man's dick! Why would you say something like that?" Her open hand came upside my head right above my ear. I tried to cover my head and duck, but we had rules.

"Stand up, or I'll make this worse! I'll teach you not to talk that way! You're already a whore! Talking about sucking the dick of every 'Tom, Dick and Harry!'" Her hand kept hitting the side and back of my head until I fell to the floor crying.

It wasn't until I was fifteen and at a friend's house where I stumbled upon a book about puberty and growing bodies and realized that my mother thought of our bodies and sex differently than most. I wasn't a whore, not even close. My body wasn't sinful. I was "normal."

WHAT DO YOU TELL YOUR FRIENDS?
NORMA

When I sit around and talk with friends about family or scroll through my social media and see updates, pictures, and reminders about our childhood memories, or more specifically one's first childhood memory, I am often told of baking cookies with grandmother or sewing with mom or even fishing with dad. For me, my first memory is not so happy. It's a flash grenade that shows up unexpectedly. A blinding surprise that leaves me stunned no matter how many times I see it.

The house we lived in was a rundown apartment building; this was no different than most of the places where I grew up. There were a couple of apartments downstairs and an apartment upstairs. I could not specifically recall what apartment we were in but I can tell remember what door we used to get into our place, because I would use that door to return to the sidewalk and ride my tricycle up and down the street. The building had a brick façade that is there to this day, so I am reminded every time I drive past what happened to me when I was just a toddler. My memory is one of sweat, stench, and fear.

I woke in a bed sandwiched between my mother her boyfriend at the time. They were both undressed and my mother was giggling. I could only smell something that was unfamiliar, now as an adult I know that to be the smell of sex and musk. I could smell the remnants of the morning after the party that went on way too long. The dirty, dry cigarette smell and alcohol. Not the smell of the spilled drink on the carpet that wasn't cleaned up, but the smell of alcohol that seeps through the pores of a person that had way too much to drink. The acrid smell of alcohol and sweat mixing together. I was hot, sweaty, and closed in. I slid underneath the sheet to try to wiggle myself out the end of the bed as I did this my mother said to her boyfriend, "watch out for his snake."

He laughed and took his penis in his hand and shook it in my face. "Do you want to hold the snake?" He took my hand and wrapped it around his penis and my mother laughed. I don't recall much after that. I don't know if that was the end of the memory or if I just must wait longer to recall the rest. Does it really matter? Is that not enough?

Years later that man came into the store where I worked. He slithered up to the counter to buy his beer and cigarettes. I cashed him out as I shook with fear and nerves. He winked at me and said, "Thanks babe." I see him now from time to time, more often than I'd like.

When I do, I fight the urge to scream out loud and point at him, "That man! Right there! He assaulted me!" But I have no proof, my tongue is tied and my first childhood memory a secret, until now.

THUNDER AND ENLIGHTENING
NORMA

Nothing quite smells like Chianti and pipe smoke. I have never met a bottle of Chianti that didn't look like a cheap dollar store hanging basket. I was biased, though. My mother referred to him as her "Shaman," a spiritual teacher and doctor. I knew him for what he was. A fat, bearded man who could eat, sleep and screw for free. I hid in my bedroom whenever he was around. They would put a blanket down in the living room and dance around on it while drunk on chianti and he smoked his pipe. As the liquor took over, they would do more than dance on their blanket. A preteen shouldn't have to hide from her mother's sex sounds.

The Shaman's name was "Thunder," although I'm sure it wasn't really. My mother danced around him in her paisley pleated skirts as they whooped and hollered. Every now and then she poked her head into my bedroom door and wagged a finger at me; her eyes dark with regret, regret for having had me. I knew this to be true as many times she let me know that she should have had an abortion. She'd whisper in a quiet voice, between her tightly gritted teeth, reminders that I better not screw things up for her. As soon as she turned back to him her voice would lilt and fly.

I felt so small. So invisible. Yet, my body was safe when he was around. He didn't hurt me, and my mother was too busy entertaining his body to turn her hands to mine. At that age I wasn't sure which abuse was easier to process. Her words cut deep, and her hands bruised hard. But sometimes, it was so nice to not feel those hands.

Hiding in my room wasn't enough; I had to go deeper. A closet, a walk-man, and notebooks. Drowning out the sounds of her sex. Drowning out the sounds of a growling stomach. Drowning out the sounds of the children upstairs laughing.

I transcribed songs on the radio into my notebook. I played, recorded, replayed, and listened again until each word was perfect. There were no search engines to do a lyric search, so I wrote. I wrote my heart out. Crying as the lyrics poured out of me onto my notebook, word by word, page by page and book by book. I kept

Beauty in Disrepair

these notebooks all through grade school and high school. They guided me when I was lost.

I still do it sometimes. When I panic and I'm scared and it seems like the walls are closing in I'll curl myself into a ball around the rubber smell of the soles of shoes; hiding my tear-stained face behind the dresses that hang low. I'll close my eyes and hear the whoops and hollers and try to drown them out with the lyrics that live in my head.

Many years and notebooks later I came home to find my mother had thrown them all away. One of her manic cleaning episodes had won that day. In the end, though, I had written all the songs on my mind.

OUR FINAL THOUGHTS

MOM
CELIA

Clinical.
Back then, they called it
Multiple Personality Disorder—
at least twenty in her head.
I met a few.
She was only a toddler when he raped her.

An angry bitch, biting teeth—
dig-mark lessons on my forearms.
Protector of the child-alter,
voracity of a Mother Bear.
I hid those marks with long sleeves,
told lies to school nurses and playmates.

An old man, strange and persuasive,
told Mom to shave her head once.
She did.
It took months to grow back.
Her pretty blue eyes, vacant.

A younger woman—
shopaholic—we had no food except
bread and grape jelly.
But man, she had the "cutest" handbag collection.

The promiscuous one—
lots of men came to visit,
lots of men *came*.
I heard their grunts as they
mounted Mother Bear.

Beauty in Disrepair

Stale beer, cigarette smoke …
dank, musky air.

A budding scholar.
4.0 GPA
She could have been great.
But she lied, made up stories.
Or *they* lied, those fetid voices.
The lies travelled, too …
every time they travelled, we moved.
New school. New friends. New lies.
Lie pretty girl, lie. Mommy is so proud of you.

But in her youth—voted most popular.
Top of her graduating class …
listening to songs of protest.
And she gave me poetry,
loved books, learning.
Gave me her eyes, too, sometimes—blistering azure.
But those eyes could go black,
like a goddess,[4] who chomped up
her children into bits.
Otherworldly.

And her voice, too,
tangled, husky, bitter
as summer crab apples or
coarse as flaking birch.
Then hushed, like that little
girl rocking herself,
playing with broken dolls
missing their glass eyes.

---

[4] This is a loose reference to Medea, who really consumed her children according to the myth.

She loved me.
She beat me.
Pretty hairbrush-bristle-wounds
felt like tiny swords.
My battle marks.
Pink flesh
tattooed with *sins of our fathers* ...
I was the Devil's child and
my father, gone.
Her words
cut like scissors:
sharp.

Still, I wove my way through
her collaged psyche,
found the pretty sway of
evergreens and swiftly
running waters.
We sent her
ashes through
rivers, buried in valleys
and cold trails.

Her soul has been released
to the wind—reclaimed and
redistributed in her
Mother Earth—
the only place
she ever called "home."

Her spirit wanders
and her voices
converge in the
soft dampness of Spring.
And we are both free.

Beauty in Disrepair

THE YOUNGEST
NORMA

Recently, my son asked me if I loved my mother. I replied that I did love her, some of her, in my own way and am beginning to love her more over time now that she is gone. It's easier to begin healing when the abuser is no longer around. Although my mother could no longer physically hurt us, she was always verbally and mentally abusive long after she stopped beating us and those wounds will heal but will leave scars.

I'm also angry with her, but for something that most wouldn't think. I'm angry that she didn't teach me how to be a mother. Angry about not knowing how to maintain a completely healthy sexual relationship, although I am learning and will always be learning these things moving forward. My real anger lies where I feel I was let down by people who were mentally fit and healthy yet did nothing to completely remove my sister and I from such an environment.

Some of these people I've spoken to about it, some I haven't. There are sometimes excuses about not having resources, not knowing how bad it was, and that it was a different time. I call bullshit, but then again, we all are only capable of doing what we know. I did have some people who stepped in; a family from one of our churches who took me in for a month as a teenager just to give me some rest. The mother of one of my best friends showed up at our apartment one day and fought for me, really fought for me. I don't even remember what she said, but I do remember standing there in awe as this mother stood there pleading a case as to why I was worth of better treatment The only other person who had ever done that before was my sister. These people were few and far between.

I wouldn't have made it through my younger years if not for a surrogate family who had stepped in and helped my mother when she needed it. Or the friend I had made at as a toddler. We saw kindergarten together, our first children born within three weeks of each other, and have seen each other through some pretty hard times and some great ones. We're still best friends.

I wouldn't have made it through high school without a couple of girlfriends who probably don't realize the impact that they had on my life. They gave me songs to sing to and Mondays to look forward to; boys to talk about and cars to drive in. One young man who I was in class with lived nearby me; we occasionally met up on the walk home from school. He had met my mother on a few occasions and had something of a clue I believe. One of the few who did. He'd always look me in the eyes before we parted ways and I went into my house. He asked me, "You got this?" I'd nod and be on my way. I didn't have it, but just knowing someone cared helped. I can count on both hands the ones that stepped in to really help me. I would like to curse the ones who never did, but I'd rather use my energy to praise the ones that did.

There were aspects of my mother's personality that were peaceful or benign; some that were even loving or caring. The small children, however kind, still weren't capable of taking care of us. Buying coloring books, crayons and ice cream didn't pay the bills. The teenager could be fun. I spent one of my birthdays at a local bar with my mother listening to a band and drinking mudslides. Then there was the nurse. She would spend hours during my menstrual cycle helping me to clean my sheets and change my bed as I suffered from excessive bleeding.

There was one alter that I had always hoped was my true mother. The one who birthed me, fed me, clothed me, and fought for me. The one who fended off grabby boyfriends and shielded me from an abusive father. The mother who scraped together pennies for Easter baskets and Sunday dresses and the one who cared if we were home by the time the streetlights came on and put sunscreen on us. I always wanted this mother, but she was only around sometimes, but those sometimes did count.

That mother would wake me in the middle of the night when she got home from working at the hospital. She would take out a package of peanut butter cookies that she had stolen off a patient's tray. Two in a package. The gold packaging looked so good and the smell of the fresh cookies as she opened the cellophane wrapper is something I can still smell to this day. We each had a cookie. She told me about work. I talked about the neighbor's water slide or backyard pool and after she tucked me back in and kissed my forehead. I dreamt of that mother. I still do. This is how I try to remember her.

THE OLDEST
CELIA

Although we have a lot of healing yet to do, we are in much healthier places than we have been. We are both in stable, happy marriages, continue to write as our catharsis, and to share our experiences for those who understand what we have been through. We did not share these stories to hurt any of our family or friends, for they sustained us in times we may not have known they were doing so, and as best they could at particular moments in our lives. I had several families in one of our churches that stepped in to rescue me, if only for short periods of time. I spent a summer with one family, a high school semester with another, and spent evenings at yet another. I am grateful to those families, who I will not name in this book to protect their privacy, for I know they did not step in to be recognized; they did it for me because they loved me as a daughter. I am grateful to them all.

Our mother, who died years ago, is finally at peace. I believe that when she passed, all alters were merged and Mom was her truest self in death. It was almost an immediate forgiveness that I was able to afford her finally, but only in her death. We know that our mother, the main personality, was an intellectual, an artist, a writer, a nurse, and a kind woman. We know that her actions were usually not her own, but rather, those of the alters that developed out of necessity to protect her child-victim self. Some were abusive physically, some were horribly cutting verbally, and others were sexually promiscuous or prudish. Still others socially ostracized us with religion and/or moving from place to place—even isolation at times. Now I do things on my own terms. I do not pretend to have all the answers; nor do I believe that I have remembered every account of abuse within this book. I recollected what I remembered. The things that happened to me were real and have shaped who I have become today. In fact, because of these experiences, I was strong enough to pursue and complete a doctoral degree—something I know Mom hoped I would achieve. She loved poetry and painting—she was truly a brilliant and creative woman. I also recall many gifts under the Christmas tree and sleepovers with best friends that Mom personally organized for us. One night she stayed up with me—literally almost all night—to help me write a paper. She earned that A+. She did the best she could.

I feel closer to a place of acceptance, I know that I forgave Mom immediately in her death, and I can help others who know the heartache of childhood trauma. But the work continues, and the healing is long and difficult. I will never forget what has been done to us, whether it was abuse, neglect, or instability. I do forgive our abuser(s), though, as I know each fought demon of their own. I do not believe that we go through trauma simply for the sake of suffering. I believe that we go through trauma to develop empathy and to guide others through the process of healing, recovery, and happiness. May all who have read this book find true peace and comfort. It will get better, we will get through this, and we are all survivors.

A POEM BY OUR MOM

HE ASKED ME TO SAY MY PRAYER

My name is: Dancing Deer.
I dance for love.
I dance for awareness.
I dance for the moment.
I dance to see.
I dance like a deer.
I dance to feel the ground.
I dance to be free,
I dance to grow,
I dance to disappear.
I dance for life
… I am Dancing Deer

Beauty in Disrepair